FANtastic Franchises
SUPER MARIO BROS. FRANCHISE

Kenny Abdo

Fly!
An Imprint of Abdo Zoom
abdobooks.com

abdobooks.com

Published by Abdo Zoom, a division of ABDO, P.O. Box 398166, Minneapolis, Minnesota 55439. Copyright © 2025 by Abdo Consulting Group, Inc. International copyrights reserved in all countries. No part of this book may be reproduced in any form without written permission from the publisher. Fly!™ is a trademark and logo of Abdo Zoom.

Printed in the United States of America, North Mankato, Minnesota.
052024
092024

Photo Credits: Alamy, AP Images, Everett Collection, Getty Images, Shutterstock
Production Contributors: Kenny Abdo, Jennie Forsberg, Grace Hansen
Design Contributors: Candice Keimig, Neil Klinepier, Colleen McLaren

Library of Congress Control Number: 2023948540

Publisher's Cataloging-in-Publication Data

Names: Abdo, Kenny, author.
Title: Super Mario Bros. franchise / by Kenny Abdo
Description: Minneapolis, Minnesota : Abdo Zoom, 2025 | Series: FANtastic franchises | Includes online resources and index.
Identifiers: ISBN 9781098285609 (lib. bdg.) | ISBN 9781098286309 (ebook) | ISBN 9781098286651 (Read-to-me eBook)
Subjects: LCSH: Nintendo video games--Juvenile literature. | Super Mario Bros. (Game)--Juvenile literature. | Adventure video games--Juvenile literature. | Video games industry--Juvenile literature. | Branding (Marketing)--Juvenile literature. | Popular culture--Juvenile literature.
Classification: DDC 338.768--dc23

TABLE OF CONTENTS

Super Mario Bros. 4

Origins 6

Through the Years. 10

Fandom 20

Glossary 22

Online Resources 23

Index 24

SUPER MARIO BROS.

Starring in more than 200 video games, their own TV shows, and movies, the Super Mario Bros. are super in more ways than one!

ORIGINS

Nintendo game designer Shigeru Miyamoto released *Donkey Kong* in 1981. Players controlled the character Jumpman. The goal was to save a lady who had been kidnapped by a big gorilla named Donkey Kong.

1UP
HIGH SCORE
003700   **007650**

L=00

BONUS
4300

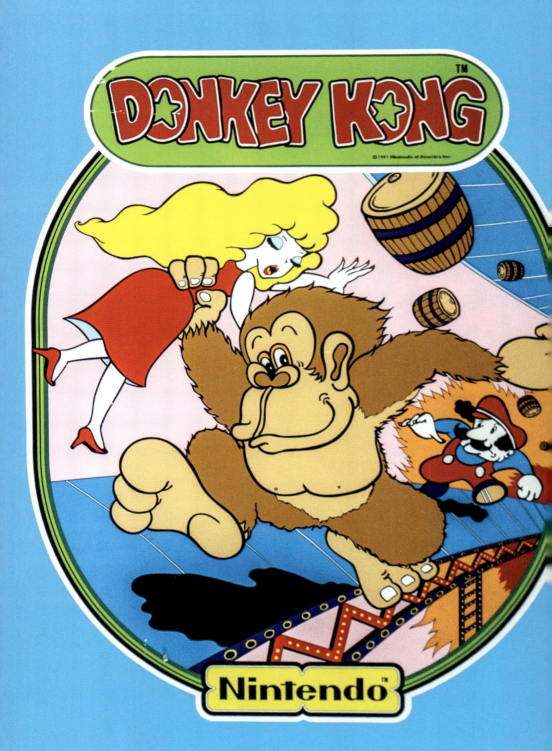

Donkey Kong was a huge hit. It led to many **sequels** and **spin-offs**. However, the biggest surprise success came from the game's playable character who could only jump.

THROUGH THE YEARS

Miyamoto changed Jumpman's name to Mario. This honored Mario Segale, Nintendo of America's office landlord. Now, Mario just needed a partner for his adventures!

Miyamoto gave Mario a brother named Luigi. *Ruiji* means "similar" in Japanese. Miyamoto felt that Luigi was similar to Mario. Only he was taller and donned green gear.

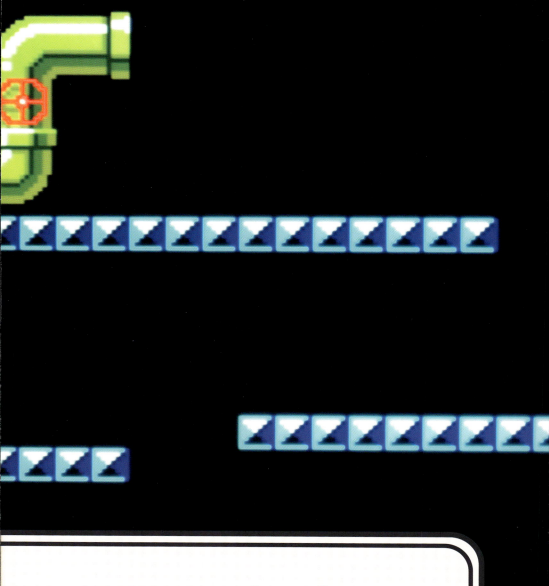

Mario Bros. made its **debut** in 1983. Released for **arcades** in the United States, it was quickly popular with gamers. Soon, Mario and Luigi arrived in homes around the world.

In 1985, *Super Mario Bros.* was released on the Nintendo Entertainment System (NES). It introduced fan favorites like Princess Peach, Bowser, and the Goombas. It also established gameplay items such as Fire Flower, Super Mushroom, and Invincibility Star.

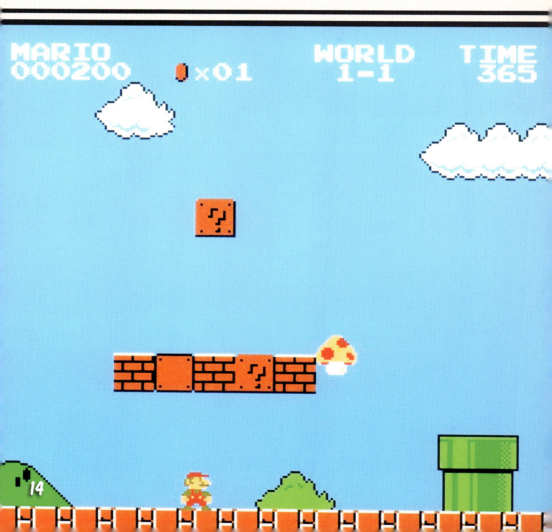

Mario Bros. fever took over the world. Mario and Luigi appeared on all types of merchandise. The duo had clothing, toys, and cereal. They were also regularly featured in *Nintendo Power* magazine.

Mario and Luigi have jumped to each Nintendo **console**, from the N64, to the Wii, and the Switch. The **franchise** also dipped into different genres. They included racing, party, and role-playing games.

Mario and Luigi also made the leap onto big and small screens. In 1989, *The Super Mario Bros. Super Show!* **debuted**. In 1993, the **live-action** movie, *Super Mario Bros.*, was released. Critics did not respond well to the film, but some fans enjoyed it.

The brothers hit big-screen success in 2023. *The Super Mario Bros. Movie* became the highest-**grossing** film based on a video game after just one week! Mario and Luigi were true movie stars!

FANDOM

The Super Mario Bros. series is featured in the **Guinness Book of Records**. It claimed the record for most successful video game **franchise** of all time!

Mario and Luigi are two of the most famous characters in video game history. Miyamoto set out to make a fun game. Instead, he created the biggest **icons** of the gaming world!

GLOSSARY

arcade – an indoor space that has multiple video games to play.

console – a type of device that you play video games on.

debut – a first appearance.

franchise – a collection of related video games in a series.

grossing – earning.

Guinness Book of Records – a reference book published annually that lists world records.

icon – a person or thing that people recognize as a symbol of something and is an object of great respect and admiration.

live-action – involving real, traditional actors and cameras.

sequel – a movie or other work that continues the story begun in an earlier work.

spin-off – a movie starring a popular character in a secondary role of an earlier movie.

ONLINE RESOURCES

To learn more about the Super Mario Bros. franchise, please visit **abdobooklinks.com** or scan this QR code. These links are routinely monitored and updated to provide the most current information available.

INDEX

Bowser 14

Donkey Kong 6, 9

Guinness Book of Records 20

Jumpman 6

Luigi 11, 12, 21

Mario 10, 12, 21

Mario Bros. 12

merchandise 15

Miyamoto, Shigeru 6, 10, 11, 21

movies 17, 19

Nintendo 6, 16

Nintendo Power 15

Princess Peach 14

Segale, Mario 10

Super Mario Bros. 14

Super Mario Bros. Super Show!, The 17